THE AUTHENTIC LEADER AS SERVANT (ALS)

ALS I COURSE 1
AFFECTION LEADERSHIP
Attributes, Principles, and Practices

SYLVANUS N. WOSU, Ph.D

THE AUTHENTIC LEADER AS SERVANT
ALS I COURSE 1
Affection Leadership Attributes, Principles, and Practices

© Copyright 2024 by Sylvanus N. Wosu Ph.D.

Printed in the United States of America
ISBN: 978-1-961526-59-4

All rights reserved. No part of this book may be reproduced or transmitted in any form or by any means, electronic or mechanical, including photocopying, recording, or by any information storage and retrieval system, without permission in writing from the copyright owner.

Bible quotations are from the New King James (NKJV) version of the Bible unless otherwise indicated.

Other versions used in this book are the New International Version (NIV), New Living Translation (NLT), King James Version (KJV), English Standard Version (ESV), and Good News Translation (GNT). Unless otherwise specified, NKJV should be assumed.

The views expressed in this work are solely those of the author and do not necessarily reflect the views of the publisher, and the publisher disclaims any responsibility for them.

To order additional copies of this book, contact:
Proisle Publishing Services LLC
39-67 58th Street, 1st floor
Woodside, NY 11377, USA
Phone: (+1 646-480-0129)
info@proislepublishing.com

TABLE OF CONTENTS

FOREWORD	XI
ACKNOWLEDGMENTS	XV
DEDICATION	XVII
PREFACE	19
About Leader As Servant Leadership (LSL) Model	22
About the Authentic Leader as Servant (ALS)	25
About the ALS Courses	26

CHAPTER 1
UNDERSTANDING LEADERSHIP ATTRIBUTES   35

- Functional Definitions — 35
- Comparisons With Other Works — 40
- Principle of Leadership Attribute — 42
- Authentic Leadership Attributes — 43
- Summary 1 Understanding Leadership Process — 49

CHAPTER 2
AFFECTION LEADERSHIP ATTRIBUTE   53

- Characteristics of Affection Attribute — 54
- Principle of Affection Attribute — 54
- Practicing Affection Attribute — 55
- Summary 2 Leadership Affection Attribute — 57

CHAPTER 3
DEVELOPING THE ACTS OF AFFECTIVE-LOVE   63

- Extend practical care for the follower — 63
- Bear with the follower in love (longsuffering) — 64
- Summary 3 Developing the Acts of Affective-Love — 64

CHAPTER 4
DEVELOPING LEADERSHIP AFFECTIVE-KINDNESS   67

- Summary 4 Developing Leadership Affective-Kindness — 68

CHAPTER 5
DEVELOPING THE ACTS OF AFFECTIVE COMPASSION   71

- Use Empathetic Compassion to Give Affection — 71
- Give affection with authentic emotions — 71

Summary 5 Developing the Acts of Affective Compassion ---------------------- **72**

CHAPTER 6
DEVELOPING THE ACTS OF AFFECTIVE WORK   75

Extend and be spent for others --**75**
A Case of Affective Work --**75**
Summary 6 Developing the Acts of Affective work-------------------------------**77**

TOPIC INDEX   83
REFERENCES   85

FOREWORD

The modern world today is obsessed with standardization and modalities. As a result, in the realm of leadership, many books have spout associated leadership theories and models and explain them as the path to follow. However, the critical dimensions that distinguish the effectiveness of any leadership process are the values and attribute the leader brings to the table; desired change is influenced by leadership styles or standards. These many standards and theories of leadership often are not in step with the changing times or the followers' needs. The trend is a bit like stocking different kinds of foods in a grocery store and expecting that they will meet everybody's needs the same way and at all times. Aisles are packed with varieties of food with expiration dates in the future, but getting the best deal on the products is what really matters to those who buy and use the products

In many ways, this is the state of leadership in the modern world. Increasingly, even leaders of public institutions are tasked with turning a profit for themselves or the organization they serve. The idea of a "leader" seems to float uneasily alongside the ranks of fundraisers or profit raisers in contrast to any kind of role model for followers or employees. That which is knowable, measurable, and marketable has surpassed the difficult intangibility of strong moral leadership attributes as the central guideline for achievement and success.

In this complicated space, Dr. Sylvanus Wosu introduces his complex idea of the Leader as a Servant Leadership, which is in this book, modeled on Christian tradition. Like all intricate ideas, Dr. Wosu's central point depends on a paradox: a person is best qualified to lead when he or she is most ready to serve. This paradox has been monopolized rhetorically by "public servants" who often serve either self-interest or the interests of specific lobbies. The Authentic Leader as Servant penetrates past the superficial concept of "serving" and details the internal state of true servitude or Servanthood.

While the book is primarily focused on the Christian model of leadership attributes such as discipleship, empathy, affection, and Servanthood, it does so not merely on the grounds of blind faith, but rather via numerous contemporary sociological and business-driven studies on how leaders should seek a leader-follower relationship that is simultaneously productive and nurturing. Dr. Wosu's most piercing insights always involve this secular–Christian dialogue. This book demonstrates that Christ's model for leadership is one that may exist successfully outside the confines of a faith relationship; it places the values of Christ's religious significance in leadership at the center of the framework. It is clear from Dr. Wosu's generous own life story of faith—a faith tested by humbling difficulties—is at the center of both his orientation and motivation for writing.

In language that is so concise, it is often illustrated in mathematical formulas; Dr. Wosu explains the deep structural integrity of Christ's Leader as the Servant Leadership model. One could imagine leaders of any doctrine benefiting from the analyses contained in these pages. The book's message repeatedly encourages the reader to imagine a scenario or reflect on memories and personal experiences to prove or test its many points. Thus, the book depends on a form of praxis, a lesson that could be or has been enacted, by the participating reader. I am very impressed at the volume and level of thinking of the author. Parts of the book involve his personal story, which is especially riveting. I cannot imagine what he had to endure, which he referred to as a" wilderness walk," to accomplish the goal he set for himself. His life stories on these pages are inspiring and stimulating.

In this way, the text eschews dogmatism in favor of the self-discovery Socratic Method of teaching and learning. The reader is not badgered into complying with a religious objective but is rather asked to consider the applicability of difficult biblical concepts in relation to modern life. It is a fascinating and very thought-provoking read.

Hence, the book does not seek to make the leader a servant, a cookie-cutter corporate buzzword, but rather asks the reader to imagine him or herself interacting with a range of concepts. One of Dr. Wosu's great strengths is his reservation when it comes to forcing his reading's interpretation on the material he presents.

The book parallels Biblical and modern leadership scenarios in ways that consistently provoke thought, and while it is clear Dr. Wosu has his particular leadership style; the space for the reader's own thoughts is always left open.

Foreword

The book could not have been written in any other way with integrity. Its format and formulas are offered to the reader of the leader as a servant role that it analyzes in its pages. To find a text that instructs from this humble position is profoundly refreshing in a genre that is often packaged inside a cover with a sizeable picture of the "modest" author, smiling egotistically beneath a name spelled out in large, gold lettering. Throughout its pages, this text feels as if it serves the reader.

In the end, this is the most satisfying aspect of the book. There is no standardized approach to achieving successful leadership. There is no promise of power and a bigger payday; in fact, the book often proffers just the opposite. The reader is not encouraged to devalue the experience of leadership by finding some economic metric for marking success but is rather asked to think deeply about the most basic elements of internal and social interaction within the framework of a Christian tradition. What this means will be different for every reader. Indeed, even in the context of single chapters, I found myself questioning or re-evaluating moments of my own life. This book serves; it doesn't feel like filling in multiple-choice questions, staring at a wall of flavorless grocery products, or hearing the endless servant promises of today's political scene. It feels like a humble invitation to consider a single paradoxical element of a profoundly productive tradition.

-Tobias Bates

ACKNOWLEDGMENTS

A book on leadership attributes as aspects of Servant Leadership sprouted from the wealth of knowledge and the inspirations of many other leaders. Their writings were sources of inspiration, challenges, and examples of excellence to emulate.

Dr. Enefaa N. Wosu, my wife and life partner, for her love, commitment, and prayer support, especially during those long night hours I was not there for her and her constant reminder of who I must be as a leader-servant. Without her support, forbearance, wisdom, and encouragement, this project would not have been completed; I say, thank you very much.

And to God alone be all the glory and honor for the divine inspiration and guidance in initiating and completing this life-transforming book project.

DEDICATION

I humbly submit this book back unto the gracious hands of God who inspired the writings through His Holy Spirit!

I dedicate this book to my virtuous wife of 45 years, Rev. (Dr.) Enefaa Wosu whose spiritual leadership is an important gateway to our home, and to our four wonderful children—Prof. Eliada Wosu-Griffin EL, HeCareth, Tamuno-Emi, and Chidinma. From them all, I learnt what it meant to be a leader-servant. I could not be blessed with better teachers.

PREFACE

What characteristics did Biblical leaders like the Apostle Paul, Moses, Joshua, and Nehemiah as servants of their people display outwardly that distinguished them from other leaders, both then and now? The Apostle Paul kept his focus to *emulate* Christ and endured all the infirmities and persecutions he suffered to complete his goal to preach the gospel of Jesus Christ. He inspired Timothy and others through his effective *discipleship* leadership to imitate him as he emulated Christ. Moses' outward display of his *trus*t in God's power earned him a good level of trust from the people and empowered him for the mission of delivery of God's children from bondage in Egypt; he had to *reproduce* himself in Joshua to complete the mission. But the greatest of them was Jesus Christ, who humbly sacrificed His life to finish the work of redemption. In His *Servanthood*, commitment, and love for the people, He became the ultimate *model* of a leader as a servant to *emulate*.

Let's consider for a moment secular leaders in these current times! For example, think of Henry Ford, who founded the successful Ford Motor Company; Bill Gates who created the global empire that is Microsoft; Albert Einstein, who in many ways is synonymous with a genius for his contributions to modern physics; Abraham Lincoln, remembered as one of the greatest presidents and leaders of United States; and many others like these we cannot mention. What did all these leaders have in common? What propelled them to turn their initial failures or challenges into eventual successes? None had a direct mentor or inherited any fortune from their parents. Nevertheless, they all eventually succeeded. These people can be distinguished from others based on their self-will to succeed, their self-confidence and belief in themselves, their self-determination, and their perseverance, among other characteristics. The distinguishing characteristics displayed externally in service or relationships toward others are the outward functional attributes that define that leader.

Think about yourself as a student, faculty member, or that new executive. What was it that made your journey to success different and even great? Students and colleagues, when they see or hear about my display of what I have referred to as the 'wilderness walk of faith', have asked me to share the critical attitudinal elements that made me remain inwardly resilient and undaunted and yet outwardly joyful in the difficulties I had faced. This book is the result of those reflections. Let me explain one such teaching moment.

Many years ago, sitting in my research lab on a Saturday morning trying to finish writing my dissertation, a fellow graduate student walked into the room to talk with me. He was contemplating terminating his graduate studies. He was a privileged single male student but felt the load was just too much.

"Sylvanus," he asked, with seriousness in his eyes, "your research advisor suggested that I should ask you, 'what is it that makes you tick?'.'What is it about you that makes you joyful and at peace with yourself and determined to finish, no matter the situations and high expectations we face in this department?"

What he asked me were deeply reflective questions, but I was willing and excited to answer them. Even so, before I do, let's look at the context. At that period in my life, I had four little children as a graduate student; in fact, more children than any of the faculties at that time, except for one faculty member who had eight children. I received little or no support from the department. I was then an international alien, did not qualify for financial aid, and was not given any research assistant position. I was, therefore, self-supported with two off-campus part-time jobs. I joked at being a minority of minorities, the only student in the department with such a label,—but I was self-willed to succeed. My adaptability attribute, coupled with perseverance and resilience, was all that I needed to succeed despite the odds against me. In every exam, homework assignment, or project I had to compete with students with full financial aid, plus they had nothing to distract their attention from their studies. I lived with the attitude that using disadvantages as an excuse was not an option. Aspiring to earn my Ph.D. was a life dream, and I was willing to give my ultimate best to actualize that dream even in the face of challenges. The choice was mine!

So I looked at my classmate and all I could see was a student striding through a valley through which I also walked. He needed me to show him how to walk the walk, to empathize with him. To answer his question, I smiled, not that I wanted to, but because it was just who

I was. The joy he attributed to me was an overflow of my appreciation of God's grace that His life in me was externally manifesting His light to bless someone else. It was a great teaching moment; I capitalized on it to tell my classmate that my joy was not about me. He could see physically but about He who was in me, he could not see in the flesh; I needed him to know that I was just showing forth His life in me. At first, my classmate did not understand the spiritual prose or metaphor I was using. He looked surprised but open to hearing more.

I did not ask if he was a Christian. However, right on my desk was my small green pocket Bible. I opened to 2 Corinthians 12:9 (NIV) and handed it to him to read. As he read the passage: "But he said to me, 'My grace is sufficient for you, for my power is made perfect in weakness.' Therefore, I will boast all the more gladly about my weaknesses, so that Christ's power may rest on me," I noticed how absorbed he was in the words

He looked astonished and read it again, this time silently. "This is interesting, but what does this mean?" He asked. I took his question to mean, "How does this relate to my question?

I explained to my friend that the external attitudes he or my advisors saw in me that warranted the question, "What makes you tick" were inspired by my inner value system based on my faith in this same Christ and His teachings. My desire to manifest His life and self-confidence is all because of what He has promised in His word if I believed. I have believed His words and have gained self-determination and faith to make the right choices through Him for my life, and his spirit has given me perseverance and resilience to focus on finishing strong in pursuit of any goal. "With that faith, I have continued, more passionately and excitedly; I can look at my challenges and vulnerabilities and delight joyfully in them, even as an alien minority of minorities! His grace and power have empowered me to do all things I want to do. That is what makes me tick," I explained.

He looked at me as if he got his answer. "Wow, thanks!" he said, looking inspired and ready to face his challenges. As we concluded with a prayer, and he stood up to leave, I pointed empathetically to his face and said, "If I made it despite my challenges, you have absolutely no excuse but to persevere to complete your studies; you can make it too!"

It is fitting to report that this encounter with my classmate transformed his will and determination to continue. Yes, he was encouraged and went on to complete his graduate studies. He emulated self-will and perseverance from the example of the most vulnerable of all students in the department.

The inner value system of a Leader-Servant is founded not only on his faith but his self-will, coupled with self-leadership; it is the greatest mentor who can turn any situation into an inconceivable success. Self-will is the primary driver for determination, resilience, and perseverance. It is what wakes you up in the morning to ask for strength to do whatever it is you are setting out to do. Based on my life walk of faith, I can state with absolute certainty that faith is the unseen assuredness that can empower you to turn your life's probable impossibilities into great and improbable possibilities.

ABOUT LEADER AS SERVANT LEADERSHIP (LSL) MODEL

Looking at the testimony above, do you know the source that energizes the characteristics you display outside and how your inner self is related to what others see outside? What distinguishes you from others is what combines to define your attributes! As a follower, can you identify the characteristics that distinguish your leaders? As an executive, how do you base your evaluation of yourself? Or how do you evaluate that brand-new manager or new youth director you want to hire? To what do you compare the individual's qualities when you look at his CV? What is the basis of your measure? Do you know if you are a substantial leader? These personal questions and much more are the subjects of this two-volume book, 'The Authentic Leader as Servant Part I: The Outward Leadership Attributes, Principles, and Practices', is written in two parts; the second part 'The Leader as Servant Leadership Model. Part II'; deals with the Inner Strength Leadership Attributes, Principles, and Practices.

When we think about today's corporate greed, deepening divide between the haves and have-not, gridlock in political systems, conflicts and wars, high divorce rates, and the rich young ruler in the Bible, it is easy to agree that all these people share a few things in common: self-centeredness, pride, lack of compassion, and greed. There is a great need in today's suffering world for leader-servants who display leadership attributes. These attributes should be oriented toward selfless service to others. Indeed, our world is increasingly drifting away from global serving reality toward the self and apathy. The most credible message or model for a possible solution to this dilemma and the answer to several complex leadership questions can be found in the foundation of the ultimate leader-servant, Jesus Christ. This book defines the Leader as Servant Leadership attribute as the combined acts of two or more distinctive functional leadership characteristics exhibited in service and relationship toward others. There is no better time than now for a book that presents comprehensive and irrevocable facts and principles regarding how to develop effective attributes of the leader-servant.

The Leader as Servant Leadership Model

My first book on this subject, The Leader as Servant Leadership Model, explains that Jesus' servant leadership model is based on the notion of a Leader as a Servant and not on a Servant as Leader. There are four distinct differences between a Servant as Leader (Servant-leader) and the Leader as Servant (leader--servant) models. It is pertinent to highlight them here to connect to this book, Authentic Leader as Servant.

A Leader as Servant is a leader first. The leader–servant as a leader does not in the line of duty go projecting or lording his or her power and authority over others but is the person to lead the process of influencing desired changes in others through his humble example of being a servant or having a serviceable attitude toward others. He or she is a serving leader, not a lording leader. He leads as a servant by putting others' needs above his own needs and rights. Jesus emphasized the word "as" meaning that the leader (the Master) chooses to serve as a servant even though he is the leader. A leader–servant emulates Jesus, who gave up all rights, and emptied and expended Himself on His followers. He empowered them to become more like Him. A leader-servant is known as a leader first but is seen as a great leader by his humble attendant heart and acts of service to others. His greatness comes from his ability to put others above himself.

Leader as Servant is a Biblical Concept. The model or image of a humble serving leader motivated Jesus' disciples to see that if their master could do this for them, they must also be able to do it for others. Jesus clearly demonstrated the process of leader-as-servant leadership. In some cases, He chose to serve by leading when He wanted to create the image or model of the leader-servant in certain acts. In other cases, He chose to lead by serving, when he showed care and empathy toward the people and led the disciples to see empathy as a leadership attribute.

Leader as Servant is an Authentic Leadership Model to follow. The Leader as the Servant leadership model intentionally positions Jesus as an original model of a leader to follow.

He was serving His disciples to demonstrate that the process of becoming a great leader was earned through humble acts of service to others; He made them understand that He was empowering them to succeed Him as leader-servants through service to others. The result was an incomparable legacy of leadership that changed their communities. The fact that Jesus relinquished his rights or shared His power did not diminish His power and influence. In fact, his influence increased at least 11 X 100%, if we ignore the one case of Judas.

The Leader as Servant Transforms Organizational Culture. The proposed LSL model seeks to transform and sustain the community or organization by instilling key leadership values or "leadership presence" among followers or an organization's members. Change is sustained when everyone in the organization takes ownership of the change. Rather than focusing on leading more followers to be great followers who conform to the organizational culture, LSL seeks to lead and empower better leaders to be distinguished leaders and community builders.

There are four distinctions, which clearly differentiate many of the existing servants as Leader-based philosophies in relation to servant leadership from my LSL model. Even in the corporate or institutional worlds, there is nothing better than Jesus on which to base Servant Leadership. There is nothing more authentic and impacting than the servant leadership modeled by the life and teachings of Jesus Christ.

The LSL model uses exploratory questions, scenarios, and graphic visualizations to excite critical thinking in ways no other book on this subject has yet attempted. Several personal testimonies of my wilderness walk of faith with God are used to connect the reader to real-life experiences of the concepts discussed. The riveting effect is that the text engages and encourages the reader to walk through the experiences presented. The aim is to inspire the reader spiritually, mentally, and professionally with this far-reaching exposition on the subject of servant leadership.

ABOUT THE AUTHENTIC LEADER AS SERVANT (ALS)

The *Authentic Leader as Servant* argues that no leadership model is as authentic, other-centered, able to build communities, and productive and service-oriented as the model of our ultimate leader-servant, Jesus Christ. No source can provide a better point of reference than that provided in the Bible. Hence, this book aims to be more than just a text on leadership; it hopes to be a personal discovery for those who aspire to develop effective leadership attributes that grow leaders as servants who ultimately develop thriving other-centered communities. This book presents a comprehensive, biblically-based study regarding how to develop these attributes and how they are applied in a servant leadership process. In this biblical context and for clarity, Servant Leadership means *Leader-as-Servant Leadership*. A *leader-servant* refers to a *leader as a servant*, which is distinct from a servant-leader or servant as leader.

Leader as Servant Leadership attributes are shaped by the Leadership's Inner Value system, which consists of character, motivation, and commitment. The *Authentic Leader as Servant* is presented as a necessary resource to complement my *The Leader as Servant Leadership (LSL) Model*. The LSL model integrates a transformative leadership framework and interactive dimensions of Servant Leadership. Leader as Servant Leadership is a process in which a leader, in his leadership position, purposefully chooses to put others' rights and needs above his positional rights and personal needs. He then serves, enables, and empowers followers for growth that builds a thriving organization. The LSL model looks at the predominant Servant Leadership concepts and shares how they compare with biblical principles on how we should lead and be led.

ABOUT THE ALS COURSES

The three books, *LSL Model* and *The Authentic Leader as Servant (*Parts I and II), together demonstrate that with today's global visions to reach people of all races and cultures, now is the time for an authentic servant's heart of service. Those visions and the leadership processes are most effective with the appropriate leadership attributes centered more on people than on the organization, principles regarding how to develop effective attributes of leader-servant.

The ALS I and II combined presented twenty leaders as servant leadership attributes. The series of ALS courses supply training guide to understand, develop, and practice the attributes in a leadership process. Each course is independent and self-contained and does not depend on completing any other course in the series of 20 courses. It is, however strongly recommended, in fact a must read, that chapters 1 and 2 in each series be covered as they lay the foundation of LSL model on which ALS is based.

ALS (Parts I & II) Course Layout

The *Authentic Leader as Servant (ALS)* leadership (parts I and II) book has been broken down into 20 courses in workbook format to achieve three goals 1) Self-discovery of the acts of developing the attribute under review in the course, 2) deeper understanding of the principles, research and biblical teaching behind the attributes, and 3) Learning the strategies for practicing the attributes.

Instruction

The set of questions following each chapter are designed to serve as a guide to discover, explore, and practice the essential ALS leadership attributes, principles, and practices in leadership process. The questions are comprehensive review based on the content of this specific chapter only.

To maximize the learning outcomes, the learner must read through this chapter and sections. Some referenced scriptures in the book are repeated in the summaries for added review if needed, even though they were discussed in the section in which they apply.

> The exercises that follow each chapter will help you in not only understanding your own strength and weaknesses in your acts of the attribute but will guide you in developing practical strategies you can apply in self-leadership process or helping others grow in leadership
>
> All answers to the questions are contained in the associated chapter or sections; consultation of new sources, except for the reference scriptures, is not needed. Thus, it is expected that you answer the questions after you have read the associated section or chapter of the workbook. The scripture or other references cited are only for references as they already discussed in the book

ALS I Couse 1: Affection Leadership Attribute—*Affection flows from a person to produce positive emotions for the well-being of another person.*

An average person will define the word "love" in the sense that affection is a characteristic of love. Nevertheless, that definition clouds the functional meaning of affection as an attribute of a leader-servant. Affection is a love action intentionally given to someone to create favorable emotion. We experience a positive emotion when we receive or give affection. In his acts of affection, the Apostle Paul communicated to the Corinthian Christians how he spoke to them freely with an open heart, because it was an important way to give affection (2 Corinthians 6:11-13). He also spoke of longing for them with the affection of Jesus Christ (Philippians 1:8); an affection that needs to be mutual (1 Peter 1:7). How is the affection leadership attribute an outward leadership attribute? This course explores this and other questions to discover the characteristics of affection attributes and to formulate a functional principle based on the expected outcome of affection and the effective use of these attributes in leadership.

ALS I Course 2: Discipleship Leadership Attribute- *Discipleship transforms and empowers followers for service leadership that grows communities.*

Discipleship as an act of developing a follower toward a specific goal is an important function of leadership to equip others to lead. *Discipleship transforms and empowers followers for service leadership that grows communities*. A disciple is a follower who willingly chooses to follow the master and submits to his discipleship and authority. In that regard, Jesus wanted all his followers to be his disciples and ambassadors because a disciple is always a follower. Organizationally, a follower could be a junior employee, any employee in a brand-new department, a new younger faculty, or just any person that needs to be guided through a journey of professional growth and good success. This course focuses on the general growth of followers through the acts of discipleship and presents the critical characteristics of discipleship as a leadership outward attribute. Functional definitions of leadership discipleship attributes and its principle will be presented based on those characteristics. Each characteristic will be discussed in detail with emphasis on strategies of how they can be further developed or practiced as a part of the servant leadership process.

ALS I Course 3: Emulation Leadership Attribute—*A great leader-servant outwardly and positively inspires a pattern of good works for others to follow.*

To emulate is to strive to be like someone else or to follow someone else's example by imitating something that inspires you about that person. This course evaluates how to learn from someone good leadership qualities to develop yours. How did you use what you learned from following the footstep of your hero to grow your leadership qualities. Jesus in the scripture modeled humility and Servanthood he wanted his disciples to develop same qualities. Emulation as a leadership attribute shares some characteristics with transformative leadership, where a leader intentionally conveys a clear vision of a goal, inspires the passion for the work toward the goal, and motivates the followers to follow. As a leader, how do you model a characteristic behavior for someone to follow or develop? How is Leadership Emulation Leadership Attribute an outward leadership attribute? This course explores this and other questions to discover the characteristics of affection attributes and to formulate a functional principle based on the expected outcome of effective use of these attributes in leadership.

ALS I Course 4: Generosity Leadership Attribute: *Generosity is an outward measure of the level of sacrifice, what is shared, or the impact a giving makes, not just the size of the giving*

Generosity can be defined as "the *habit of giving* without expecting anything in return. It can involve offering time, assets, or talents to aid someone in need." Such habits can include spending your personal money, time, and/or labor for the welfare of others or expending (suffering or being consumed or spending) for others' well-being. When political leaders or Board members 'vote their conscience' on important issues that affect others, what is that "conscience" and how do such leaders contribute to the welfare of others? How can you, "Do all you can, with what you have, in the time you have, in the place where you are" for the betterment of humanity All giving to help humanity is crucial to help meet the needs of the most vulnerable of God's children, as demonstrated by God as attribute of God, In this course, we will explore what distinguishes a leader's act of giving from his inside intentions. The key leadership characteristics of generosity will be discussed with respect to Servant-Leadership generosity Attributes and Principles and the details how a leader-servant can develop those characteristics and then effectively practice service leadership.

ALS I Course 5: Healing-Care Leadership Attribute: *Comforting others in any trouble with the comfort with which God comforts us, brings healing - wholeness*

What is healing Care and what does it mean in practical terms to you as a leader? Effective leadership begins with an emotionally and spiritually healthy leader who can reconcile and bring comfort to the followers, irrespective of followers' feelings (good or bad) toward the leader. The healing attribute and personal security complement each other. You must have the capacity for self-healing and individual security if you are to meet others' comforts. Personal security provides the infrastructure to support leaders in adversity and heal others that are hurting. A leader's or a group's success is measured by the strength of the weakest member or follower in the group or team.. Healing is one of the most abstract and least understood attributes in leadership, and yet one of the most important. The key distinguishing characteristics will be explored to formulate a working definition and principle of leadership healing-care attributes based on those characteristics. Each characteristic will be discussed in detail with emphasis on strategies of how they can be further developed or practiced by a leader-servant as part of the servant leadership process.

ALS I Course 6: Influence Leadership Attribute-*The true measure of leadership success in affecting desired change in conduct, performance, and relational connections in others is influence*

Leadership is an integrative process in which a person applies appropriate (leadership) attributes to guide and influence the desired attitudinal changes in others toward accomplishing a particular goal. Eight five percent of CEOs of top companies surveyed on their climb to leadership ladder said they were "influenced by another leader," compared to 10% and 5% for "natural gifting" and "result of a crisis," respectively. When we consider influence as a servant leadership attribute, we are talking about a distinguishing leadership characteristic that displays on the outside what a leader is inside, influence takes on a deeper meaning. In this course, the key leadership characteristics of influence will be identified and explored from research to frame definitions of the Servant-Leadership influence attribute and principle. Based on those characteristics, the key outcomes of effective leadership influence 1 how a leader-servant can develop those characteristics and then effectively practice service leadership.

ALS I Course 7: Persuasion Leadership Attribute—*The means of transforming others to a new perspective is through empathetic persuasion.*

Persuasion attribute affords the leader the capacity to convince his followers or others to believe and engage in a new idea or goal through encouragement rather than using his positional authority or intimidation. Because members of the group may already have their views on an issue, the leader must carefully approach persuasion as a learning process to avoid conflicts or polarizing the group. He must unify the diversity of views to get buy-in and willingness to agree and follow. The leader-servant primarily relies on making decisions within an organization based on persuasion rather than positional authority. In other words, you will never hear the Leader-servant say, "Do it because I am the boss, and I say to." This particular element offers one of the clearest distinctions between the traditional authoritarian model of leadership and the concept of Servant leadership. In this course, we will explore the technique of convincing rather than coercing as one of the most effective ways a leader-servant can build consensus within groups. Key characteristics of persuasion leadership attribute will be found, fully discussed, and modeled from the examples in the lives of other leaders.

ALS I Course 8: Responsibility Leadership Attribute—*Great leaders produce successors for legacy and greater courses as an expected product of an effective leadership reproduction.*

In his book, *360 Degree Leader*, John C. Maxwell says, "Great leaders don't use people so they can win. They lead people so they can all lead together." Such great leaders, like Jesus, Moses, Paul, and others developed other leaders through a process of reproduction. Is it possible for leaders of today to reproduce their vision in others so that can lead and build a legacy together? The answer to this question is of course yes. However, the effectiveness of a leader duplicating his leadership qualities in a follower depends on the leadership reproduction attribute of the leader. This course explores the distinguishing characteristics of reproduction as an outward attribute in servant leadership. Functional definitions of leadership reproduction attribute and its principle will be presented based on those characteristics. Each characteristic of reproduction attributes will be discussed in detail with emphasis on strategies of how they can be further developed or practiced by a leader-servant as part of the servant leadership process.

ALS I Course 9: Servanthood Leadership Attribute— *A leader-servant is most qualified to lead when ready to serve as a servant for the growth of others.*

The last time you engaged in a practical act of service on the job, at home, church, or in your community, what were the key elements in that act of service? Did you serve because you wanted to and chose to serve? Or was it because someone asked you to? The ultimate goal is for the leader's life to positively transform many lives in his or her community of followers. Consider the New Testament teachings of Jesus, who demonstrated the ultimate Leader as Servant Leadership. Jesus equated greatness to serving unpretentiously (humbly, as would a child), and He equated leading with choosing to serve others. That is the first affirmative test of authenticity for this attribute. What were the distinguishing characteristics that enabled you to serve? How is the Leadership Servanthood an outward leadership attribute? This course will give answers and meanings to these and personal reflective questions to discover the distinguishing characteristics of The Leadership Servanthood attribute. Functional definitions of The Leadership Servanthood attribute and principle will be provided based on the identified characteristics. Readers will benefit from numerous techniques, personal examples, empirical case study, and applications of the concepts.

ALS I Course 10: Trust-Integrity Leadership Attribute—*True leadership trust produces assured trustee's confidence and readiness to follow based on the credibility, competence, and shared relational connections of the trusted.*

A study examined more than 75 key components of employee satisfaction in top leadership and found that trust and confidence was the single most reliable predictor of employee satisfaction in an organization. This course will examine the results of the above study with respect to servant leadership, and how a leader-servant increases the satisfaction of the followers in an organization. When the organization is going through some challenges, how can a leader be credible in helping the followers understand the company's mission and strategy? How can he share information on how the company or institution, or department is doing and how the followers or employees will be affected? Suppose the organization's strategy is not aligned with its inner value or character, how does the leader build trust in followers or earn trust from them? Organizational leadership trust has been defined by as "an employee's willingness to take a risk for a leader with the expectation that, in exchange, the leader will behave in some desired way." The course will examine how the element of reliance and confidence in the actions of the trusted and organization are characterized by a combination of Competence (Can they do the job?), Benevolence (Do they care about me?), and Integrity (Are they honest?).

Referenced Scriptures

A variety of Bible translations from over 11,200 original Hebrew, Aramaic, and Greek words to about 6,000 English words do exist with variations in meanings and emphases. I am not a biblical scholar and do not pretend to be one; Hence, I have avoided researching the roots of these words and personally prefer New King James Version (NKJV). I have intentionally used other translations for three main reasons; first, to allow for increased impact and alignment of words to the most desired meaning and emphasis in the concepts being addressed. Second, I wanted new and personal discovery of meanings from translations with which I have not been familiar. And third, I wanted to allow readers who may desire translations other than the NKJV the benefit of their preferred translations. Hence, in addition to the NKJV, other translations used in the book include New International Version (NIV), New Living Translation (NLT), King James Version (KJV), English Standard Version (ESV), and Good News Translation (GNT). Unless otherwise specified, NKJV should be assumed.

Sylvanus Nwakanma Wosu

CHAPTER 1
UNDERSTANDING LEADERSHIP ATTRIBUTES

Leadership attribute is the combined acts of two or more distinctive functional leadership characteristics exhibited in service and relationship toward others.

The starting point of our discussion is the understanding of the key functional definitions and concepts that describe the theme of this book. In general, 1 will define leadership as an integrative process in which a person applies appropriate attributes to guide and influence the sought-after attitudinal changes in others toward accomplishing a particular goal. Specifically, the Leader as Servant Leadership is a process in which a leader intentionally chooses to put the follower's rights and needs above his positional rights and personal needs, and serves, enables, and empowers them for desired spiritual and professional growth that builds thriving communities.

FUNCTIONAL DEFINITIONS

In the context of these definitions, I will begin the descriptions of the leadership attributes of an authentic leader-servant by offering a functional definition of Leadership Attributes, and showing how that definition differs from those of Leadership Character, Characteristics, and Traits.

Leadership Character is the sum total of personal qualities in leadership, such as honesty, values, vision, trust, and so on that make up the moral capital of the leader; Leadership character should describe who the leader is inside or the leader's basic personality traits.

The Leadership Characteristics describe the distinctive characteristics or features of a leader, such as attitudes, competencies, skills, and specific experiences that go beyond his character (personality). Leadership characteristics determine how (through skills and competencies) the leader leads or take actions in the process of leadership in any particular situation;

The Leadership traits are the distinguishing leadership characteristics of a leader (these are things that define his leadership characteristics), which differentiate from personality traits... Leadership traits are the set of characteristics that define a particular leader's leadership. This means that a leadership characteristic is a trait when it is a unique characteristic of the leader.

Leadership Attributes, unlike leadership character, characteristics, and traits, is *a leadership attribute and the combined act of two or more distinctive functional leadership characteristics exhibited in service and relationship toward others* or traits externally displayed in action toward others. All leadership attributes grow out of the leadership inner value system but can be externally displayed predominantly as an outbound or outward attribute or both:

1. **Outbound Attributes:** These are distinctive outward-bound attributes emanating from the inner strength of the leader to support external conduct in service and relationships toward others. They form the internal core functional qualities that motivate or enhance the outward manifestation of the inside character toward others. The outbound attribute such as listening and vision, for example, are the direct results of the inner values of the leader such as patience, hearing, love, humility, or all the fruits of the spirit.

2. **Outward Attributes:** These are distinctive functional outward outer visible attributes emanating from the richness of the outbound and inner values of the leader. For example, external attributes such as Servanthood, emulation/modeling, empathy, etc. are outflows from the leader who will directly impact the follower. Outward attributes can be enriched by the outbound (inner) attributes. As shown in Figure 1, the outward attributes in general form the outer core of

functional attributes in the leader as servant leadership, but they can share some overlapping functions with the outbound attributes.

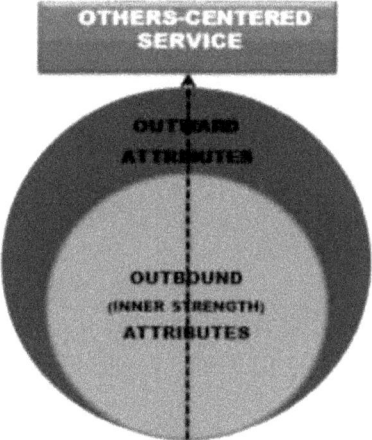

Figure 1.1. Servant leadership functional attributes

In summary, a leadership attribute is more than an ability or a characteristic; it is making those characteristics or abilities functional as part of how the leader acts (his habits) in service to others and applying those characteristics (beyond just having them) in personal and service relations to others. The character or known characteristic defines some aspects of your abilities or who you are inside— e.g. honest, humble, brave, etc. Your attribute, on the other hand, defines your habits; a display of how you use your characteristics, or the actions you exhibit toward others because of who you are inside. For example, empathy as a leadership characteristic becomes a leadership attribute if the followers can distinguish the leader's acts or habits of empathy, such as walking through with his followers in their state of suffering to bring wholeness; otherwise, it is just a characteristic or ability. Leadership attributes toward others are what impact the followers' and the organizational growth more than ability and competence.

In addressing one of the self-righteous hypocritical attributes of servitude leadership, Jesus called leader-servants to be "inside-out" leaders that reflect credibility; indeed, leaders should not appear outwardly righteous when they are full of hypocrisy and lawlessness in their hearts. He was describing "inside–out" as an authentic leadership attribute measured by the display of credibility a leadership attribute!

The measuring stick of a leader-servant is Jesus Christ. We measure ourselves unto the measure of the status of the fullness of Christ (Ephesians 4:13).

The leadership attributes of an authentic leader as a servant are encapsulated in **SERVANT/SERVING LEADERSHIP** are listed in Table 1.1, and defined in Table 1.2: *Servanthood, Emulation, Responsibility, Vision, Navigation, Adaptability, Trust, Listening, Empathy, Affection, Discipleship, Encouragement, Reproduction, Stewardship, Healing-Care, Initiation, Integrity,* and *Persuasion.* Other support attributes include *Influence, Courage, and Generosity.*

The attributes have been separated into Outward and Outbound (Inner Strength) leadership Attributes. As shown in Table 1.1, each of these attributes has three or more leadership characteristics. As such, more than 65 leadership characteristics are covered in these 20 attributes. For example, a leader's Servanthood leadership attribute is characterized by his willing servant's heart of selfless role humility, sacrifice, and submissiveness. The more these are present in a leader, the more effective the servant leadership.

Table 1.1: The functional leader-servant leadership Outbound (Inner Strength) and Outward attributes

	LEADER-SERVANT LEADERSHIP ATTRIBUTES			INNER STRENGTH ATTRIBUTES	OUTWARD ATTRIBUTES
S	Servanthood	L	Listening	Adaptability	Affection
E	Emulation	E	Empathy	Courage	Discipleship
R	Responsibility	A	Affection	Empathy	Emulation
V	Vision	D	Discipleship	Encouragement	Generosity
A	Adaptability	E	Encouragement	Initiation	Healing–Care
N	Navigation	R	Reproduction	Listening	Influence
T	Trust	S	Stewardship	Navigation	Persuasion
I	Influence	H	Healing–Care	Responsibility	Reproduction
G	Generosity	I	Initiation	Stewardship	Servanthood
C	Courage	P	Persuasion	Vision	Trust/Integrity

The list does not assume that a leader has to be excellent in all attributes or even have all of them to be an effective Leader–Servant. However, the more of these attributes the leader displays in his acts of

CHAPTER 1
UNDERSTANDING LEADERSHIP ATTRIBUTES

service toward others, the more productive he or she will be, and the further his impact on the followers and organization. The table also shows that two or more attributes can share common characteristics, which can be applied or observed in different contexts. For example, a leader's ability to inspire followers can be seen in his acts of discipleship, empowerment, an.d encouragement attributes in the context in which these attributes apply. Each attribute is exhibited either as a part of the outbound inner strength attribute of a leader or a part of the outward attribute. Table 1.1 is not an exhaustive list of attributes; in fact, there are hundreds of such attributes. This is just the starting point.

Figure 1.2: Servant leadership outward attributes (dark blue) and relationship to four foundational layers of the LSL Model

Figure 1.2 shows that the leader's attributes are shaped and secured by his four foundational layers (leadership inner value system, leadership character, motivation, and commitment). The attributes of the leader–servants are also conceptualized as the support pillars that will establish and support the personal authenticity of the leader, what the leader, does and the effectiveness of the leadership process. Thus, the attributes represent functional pillars of authentic leadership that can be learned or enriched as described in detail in the subsequent chapters. The combined effect of a secured foundation and stable support pillars will make a sustained impact on the growth of followers and the organization.

COMPARISONS WITH OTHER WORKS

The original works by Greenleaf (1970) in servant leadership [1] have been reviewed by Larry Spears (1996), who identified listening, empathy, healing, awareness, persuasion, conceptualization, foresight, stewardship, commitment to the growth of others, and building community as the ten distinguishing characteristics of servant leadership. [2] Russell (2001) has studied these attributes and have shown them to be essential in servant leadership and concluded that these qualities generally "grow out of the inner values and beliefs of individual leaders." [3] Russell and Stone (2002) extended the Greenleaf 10 attributes to 20 attributes observed in servant-leaders. These 20 attributes were categorized by these authors as either functional attributes (intrinsic characteristics of servant-leaders) or accompanying attributes (complement attributes that enhance the functional attributes).[4] The operational attributes were identified as vision, honesty, integrity, trust, modeling, service, pioneering, appreciation, and empowerment with the accompanying attributes of communication, credibility, competence, stewardship, visibility, influence, persuasion, listening, encouragement, teaching, and delegation. Only three of the attributes identified by Greenleaf were identified, and all three were accompanying attributes rather than functional. Responsibility, adaptability, affection, discipleship, navigation, and reproduction attributes which are considered critical in biblical-based servant leadership in my LSL model are not covered by Russell and Greenleaf. As shown in the description of the attributes in Table 1.2, most of the attributes reported by Russell and Stone (2002)[5] or Greenleaf [1] can be seen either in the twenty attributes or their associated characteristics. Integrity and honesty for example are leadership characteristics of trust and other attributes rather than an independent attributes. I take the position that servant leadership attributes are functional attributes in acts of duty to others and emanate from the inner value system of the leader.

CHAPTER 1
UNDERSTANDING LEADERSHIP ATTRIBUTES

Table 1.2: Description of the functional leader-servant outward leadership attributes and associated principles and characteristics

Leader–Servant Leadership Attributes	Principles of Leadership Attributes	Leadership Characteristics
Affection: *This is the combined love-based works toward providing the essential help or services for the spiritual growth or survival of another person..* (Chapter 2)	*Affection flows from a person to produce positive emotions for the well-being of another person*	Kindness Compassion Practical Love Affective signs Appreciation
Discipleship: *This is the combined acts of personally developing, intentionally equipping, and attentively empowering growth in others to reproduce a heart of service.* (Chapter 3)	*Discipleship transforms and empowers followers for service leadership that grows communities.*	Inspiring Shepherding Equipping Developing Empowering
Emulation: *This is the combined acts of initiating an authentic servant attitude as a model of service worthy of following* (Chapter 4)	*A great leader-servant outwardly and positively inspires a pattern of good works for others to follow.*	Inspiration Motivation Initiation Model Following
Generosity: *This is the combined acts of freely sharing with and giving to others as an act of kindness, without expectation of reward or return to him.* (Chapter 5)	*Generosity is an outward measure of the level of sacrifice, what is shared, or the impact a giving makes, not just the size of the giving.*	Sharing Giving Kindness Affection Love
Healing-Care: *This is the combined acts of providing comfort and empathy to make others whole emotionally and spiritually along with tending to the follower's physical and mental well-being.* (Chapter 6)	*Comforting others in any trouble with the comfort with which we are comforted by God, brings healing - wholeness.*	Self-Healing Empathy Reconciliation Comfort Relational
Influence: *This is the combined acts of positively affecting desired change in conduct,*	*The true measure of leadership success in affecting*	Model Positive attitude Authority

performance, and relational connections toward others-centered course of action or service. (Chapter 7)	desired change in conduct, performance, and relational connections in others is influence	Connection Wisdom Intelligence,
Persuasion: This is the combined acts of communicating perspective to connect, challenge, and convince with a compelling purpose to convert others to a new position. (Chapter 8)	The means of transforming others to a new perspective is through empathetic persuasion	Connecting Challenging Communicating Convincing Converting Encouraging
Reproduction: This is the combined acts of developing your leadership qualities in others and releasing them as successors to continue a greater mission. (Chapter 9)	Great leaders produce successors for legacy and greater courses as an expected product of an effective leadership reproduction.	Selecting Mentoring Equipping Empowering Releasing
Servanthood: This is the combined acts of humility, willingness, and intentionality in service to others through selfless sacrifice and submission as a servant. (Chapter 10)	A leader-servant is most qualified to lead when most ready to serve as a servant for the growth of others. The role of a leader is to serve as a servant	Servant's heart Humility Sacrifice Service Willingness Submissiveness
Trust: This is the combined acts of positive display of character, competence, credibility, and shared relational connections that produce assured trust-confidence of the trustee in the trusted. (Chapter 11)	True leadership trust produces assured trustee's confidence and readiness to follow based on the credibility, competence, and shared relational connections of the trusted.	Character Competence Integrity Credibility Confidence

PRINCIPLE OF LEADERSHIP ATTRIBUTE

In the context of servant leadership, a leadership attribute is a level above the leadership characteristic or trait of a leader. The principle of leadership attribute states that every leadership attribute has a set of distinguishing characteristics that make up the inward or outward display of the attribute. The principle reflects the essential designed purpose or outcome of the attribute or the inevitable consequence of the effective practice of the attribute. Thus, the principle of leadership attribute is a concise statement about the fundamental truth, value, or belief about the attribute in a leadership situation; it is a statement that establishes an idea about the outcome of the attribute for guiding the practical application of the attribute and its characteristics. I will postulate and frame each principle as an additive function of the characteristics of the attribute. A statement of each principle is quoted at the beginning or below the title of each chapter. It is yet to be experimentally proven if the attribute is a linear or some other non-linear function of these characteristics as variables. It is expected, however, that each character will contribute to the effectiveness of the attribute in varying degrees.

AUTHENTIC LEADERSHIP ATTRIBUTES

At a personal level, attributes are the value-based inside-out moral leadership assets that can be related to the authenticity of a leader-servant. The complexity of defining authenticity has been noted in the literature. The subject of authentic leadership is well covered in the works of Terry (1993),[5] George (2003),[6] and Shair and Eilam (2005).[7] All appear to agree that authenticity requires self-awareness and objective self-identity in personal and social interactions with others. In his book, *Advocacy Leadership*, Professor Gary L. Anderson offers individual, organizational, and societal perspectives on authenticity: "Authenticity, at a peculiar level, is living a life, whether in the private or professional term. This is congruent with one's espoused values; at the structural level, authenticity has to do with viewing human beings as ends in themselves, rather than means to other ends; at the public level, it is a state of affairs that is congruous with the shared political and cultural values of society."[8]

The basic tenets of these perspectives are very fitting to authenticity as a qualifying element of leader-servant leadership attributes. The attribute reflects how the followers see the leader based on the leader's distinctive features displayed through his or her actions personally, organizationally, and societally. The leader is seen as a leader-servant or serving leader because the followers see him lead as a servant from an inside-out value of others. This is what makes the leader authentic. Authenticity means that what a leader displays outside, in personal or leadership life of service to others, and society is based on the values the leader espouses inside.

Authenticity in servant leadership can be one or two types or both: *Outbound Authenticity and Outward Authenticity*: The Outbound (outward-bound) Authenticity is the genuineness of personal honesty from your inner strength and abilities; what you say and how you act emanate from who you are or how you feel inside. It reflects the essential truth and honesty about your outward-bound inner strength.

Outward authenticity, on the other hand, describes the truthfulness of your credibility and honesty displayed outward in relation to others; your *outer* visible behavior or how you act outwardly towards others reflects exactly your true intentions.

While *outward* authenticity is the visible *outer* indicator of the truth of who you are inside, *outbound* authenticity is outward-bound attribute from the inside of who you are. Credibility in this context is the influence a leader has to attract believability, trustworthiness, and authenticity; it is the believability, trustworthiness, and authenticity of who you are inside and outside.

A key element of personal authenticity is that it is seen or measured in the context of societal, cultural, and organizational interactions. In that context, achieving individual authenticity becomes a challenge since it is influenced by social factors and dispositions of individuals who usually depend on liberal and organizational realities. However, for leader-servant leadership, the leader can face those changing times by remaining focused on his key Biblical-based principles or *Leadership Inner Value System*. Thus, I am interested in authenticity as an essential element of effective Leader-servant leadership attributes or Leader-servant leadership attributes as drivers of leadership authenticity. With that in mind, the first critical element of authenticity in practicing or developing efficient leader-servant leadership attributes is inside-out self-examination relative to the people served rather than the organization. You may ask yourself: What will be my response when the people I lead act or react in a certain way, will it be negative or positive? What are my strengths and vulnerabilities at those times?

Professor Yacobi in his post, "Elements of Human Authenticity," noted that since "the self -arise attribute emerges from interactions between self, others, and the environment in a complex society and world, there may co-exist multiple complicated identities depending on place and context." [9] He went on to identify the following essential elements of personal authenticity: self-awareness, unbiased self-examination, accurate self-knowledge, reflective judgment, personal responsibility, and integrity, genuineness, and humility, empathy for others, understanding of others, optimal utilization of feedback from others. All of these are covered under the leadership attributes or characteristics shown in Table 1.2.

Bill George, in his book, *Authentic Leadership*, takes the position that to be an authentic leader; a person must have the following essential characteristics: [10]

- Behavior based on value: He must understand his own values and exhibit behavior to others based on those values;
- He must not compromise his values in difficult situations but could use the situation to strengthen personal values in those situations.
- Passion from a clear purpose: Be self-aware of who he is, where he is going, and the right thing to do.
- Compassion from the heart: He must lead from a compassionate heart that allows them to be sensitive to the plight and needs of others,
- Connectedness from a relationship; he must be relationally connected with people he leads,
- Consistency from the self-disciple: He must demonstrate self-discipline to remain calm, collected, and consistent in a stressful situation.

Modeled after the elements above, Table 1.3 lists six essential characteristics of authenticity for servant leadership. These fundamental characteristics cover the five identified above and can also be aligned with the leadership characteristics in Table 1.2. Each attribute in Table 1.2 is expected to pass the personal authenticity test in Tables 1.3, 1.4. In a survey of 132 Christian leaders, seventy-four percent (74%) of them agreed that they always or frequently exhibit servant leadership attributes.[11] Thus, a pass of the outward authenticity test means that a pure leader must demonstrate 70% or more of these essential elements of this legitimacy. (That is, 70% YES in the assessment questions in Tables 1.3, 1.4).

It needs to be noted, however, that a secular leader could be authentic and still lack some of the essential servant leadership attributes or characteristics such as selflessness, servanthood, and love-motivated servant attitudes of a leader-servant. Effective leader-servants are authentic leaders and personal authenticity is an essential element of leader-servant leadership. The key test for leader-servant authenticity is the quality of his inside-out value and personal character. What is most important is a change from the inside-out.

	Table 1.3: The test of essential elements of personal inner strength authenticity in servant leadership		
	Elements of Inner Strength Authenticity	**Inner Strength (Outbound) Authenticity Assessment Questions**	**YES / NO**
1	Personal inside-out value-based behavior	Are your personal inside-out values aligned with acts of service and behavior outside?	1
		Are you honest to yourself in relation to your inner strengths and abilities?	2
2	Inside-out Self-Awareness	Do you have unbiased self-examination, and accurate self-knowledge of who you are inside-out?	3
		Do you know your inner strength and weaknesses in relation to the good you want to show as an outward attribute?	4
3	Inside-out Empathy-Compassion	Do you know and feel from your inside what you want for your followers?	5
		Are you motivated to empathize, based on your inside feelings?	6
4	Inside-out Connection with followers	Do you feel deep, personal, and spiritual connection with your followers?	7
		Does what you say and how you act reflect how you feel when you relate to others?	8
5	Inside-out Emotional Self-regulation	Do you have difficulty controlling your emotion in order to remain calm in a stressful situation?	9
		Are you always able to comfort yourself?	10
6	Inside-out Authenticity Feedback	Do your followers see your inside-out value from your outside behavior?	11
		Will your followers feel that what you say you are is congruent with how you act?	12
	#YESs_____; # NOs_____: Outbound Authenticity: YES/ 12———————%		

CHAPTER 1
UNDERSTANDING LEADERSHIP ATTRIBUTES

Table 1.4: The test of essential elements of personal outward authenticity in servant leadership

#	Elements of Personal Outward Authenticity	Personal Outward Authenticity Assessment Questions	YES or NO
1	Personal value-based outward behavior	Are your personal values and beliefs aligned with your acts of service and behavior toward others?	1
		Do you live out your life according to your beliefs?	2
2	Personal Self-Awareness	Do you have clarity of your personal vision and purpose?	3
		Does what you know about yourself accurately describe what others say?	4
3	Personal Outward Empathy-Compassion	Do you apply how you feel to what your followers need?	5
		Do you lead from a compassionate heart and are you sensitive to the plight and needs of others?	6
4	Personal Connection with followers	Do you feel deep, personal connection with your followers?	7
		Does your outward action toward others reflect exactly your true intentions?	8
5	Outward Emotional Self-regulation	Do you have difficulty controlling your emotions to remain calm in a stressful situation?	9
		Does your evaluation of your value of others agree with how valued they feel?	10
6	Personal Authenticity Feedback	Do your followers see your outward acts as true and honest?	11
		Can your followers see other-centeredness in 70% or more of your attributes?	12

#YESs_____; # NOs_____; Outward Authenticity: YES/ 12---------%

Table 1.5. Leader As Servant-Leadership Audit

A servant-leader in his leadership position purposefully choses to serve and inspire acts of service in others by his example. Select and circle best answer to questions
1=Never; 2=Almost never; 3=Sometimes; 4=Frequently; 5 =Always

	Servant Leadership assessment questions	Circle no				
1	I am willing and other-centered, and readily chose to serve others as a servant for their personal growth	1	2	3	4	5
2	I model others-centered attitude in my service and relationships and inspire same for others to follow	1	2	3	4	5
3	I have a sense of obligation, willingness, and accountability for the service towards others	1	2	3	4	5
4	I have the foresightedness to specify in the present view what others' growth should be in a given future	1	2	3	4	5
5	I work toward providing the essential help or services for the spiritual growth or survival of the others;	1	2	3	4	5
6	I provide the needed purposeful course of action for how to chart the course to for my followers.	1	2	3	4	5
7	I display external credibility and a strong sense of character based on values, beliefs, and competence;	1	2	3	4	5
8	In communication, I attentively perceive and hear what is communicated, reflectively listen to understand and to be understood	1	2	3	4	5
9	I walk through with others in their state (suffering, emotions, etc.) in a way that provides the needed care and well-being	1	2	3	4	5
10	I have a measure of self-secured flexibility to adapt appropriate attitude to serve all people in different situations	1	2	3	4	5
11	I personally develop, intentionally equip, and attentively nurture spiritually growth in others	1	2	3	4	5
12	My act of bravery instills in others the courage and confidence to follow or persevere in a course of action	1	2		4	5
13	I develop my leadership qualities in others as successors to continue in a purposeful mission	1	2	3	4	5
14	I manage, maintain,, and account for all resources entrusted to me and being responsible for the difference my acts make	1	2	3	4	5
15	As a care-giver, I act to comfort and make others whole emotionally	1	2	3	4	5
16	When I see a need, I originate a vision and action, and stay committed to meet that need and desired change	1	2	3	4	5

Chapter 1
Understanding Leadership Attributes

17	I display a holistic view of an issue to inform, transform or convert others to my view through empathetic persuasion	1	2	3	4	5
18	I freely share what I have sacrificially as an act of kindness to others, without expectation of reward in return	1	2	3	4	5
19	My act of influence is to affect the actions, behavior, opinions, etc., of others based on trust, credibility and relationship	1	2	3	4	5
20	In the face challenges and danger, I act with bravery to overcome fear and take a stand with strength and conviction	1	2	3	4	5
Score Range	Add up the numbers in each column (Total Score____ Check and Understand the key areas to work on					
81-100	Strong Leader-Servant; keep it up, go and train others.					
66-80	Above average Leader-Servant; work 25% of key areas					
50-65	Average but developing; need to work on 50% of key areas					
34-49	Below average leader; work on 75% of key areas					
<34	Not a Leader-Servant; need training in all areas					

Summary 1
Understanding Leadership Process

Before starting this exercise, please read and follow the instruction in the preface of this workbook. Answers to these questions are contained in this chapter. Completion of these exercises after reading the chapter should take 60-90 minutes.

Discovering the Leadership Attributes

1. What is your alternative definition of leadership? In learning to lead, how would you differentiate the following elements:
    a. Leadership,
    b. Leader as servant leadership.
    c. Leadership characteristics.
    d. Leadership attributes
2. How should you lead in the context of this chapter?

Understanding the Leadership Principles

1. Define or state the principle of Servanthood Leadership attribute. How true is that in your leadership experience?
2. What are the key differences between the Leader as Servant and the Servant as Leader Leadership philosophies?
3. How can you display the essential qualities of authentic leader in a leadership process in challenging times.?
4. What are the characteristics of a leader-servant?
5. What was the original source of the Servant as Leader (SL)? What was the original source of Leader as Servant (LS)?
6. How do you compare the two model characters of Leo in SL and Jesus in LS
7. What is the key framework of a Leader as a Servant Leadership?

Practicing Authentic Leadership

1. Authenticity in servant leadership can be one or two types or both *Outbound Authenticity and Outward Authenticity*: Describe a time when you displayed:
    a. The Outbound (outward-bound)— *outbound* authenticity is outward-bound attribute from the inside of who you are.
    b. *The Outward Authenticity—outward* authenticity is the visible *outer* indicator of the truth of who you are inside,
2. Describe the key elements of personal authenticity seen or measured in the context of societal, cultural, and organizational interactions.
3. Take the outbound (Table 1.3) and Outward (Table 1.4) leadership authenticity tests. How (%) authentic are you (#YES/12) in each measure in your leadership process?
4. In the elements you rated as NO, review the relevant passage, learn what is missing in you and write a personal commitment statement on how to work to improve in those areas
5. How much of a leader-servant are you? Take the personal leader-servant audit in Table 1.5 to self-assess your effectiveness.
6. Based on the questions in Table 1.5, can you identify each of the twenty attributes? What ones did you score 3 ("sometimes") or less than 3? Review and learn and commit to work to improve.

CHAPTER 2
AFFECTION LEADERSHIP ATTRIBUTE

Affection flows from a person to produce positive emotions for the well-being of another person.

How do we define affection? An average person will define the word "love" in the sense that affection is a characteristic of love. Nevertheless, that definition clouds the functional meaning of affection as an attribute of a leader-servant. Affection is a love action intentionally given to someone to create favorable emotion. We experience a positive emotion when we receive or give affection. In his acts of affection, the Apostle Paul communicated to the Corinthian Christians how he spoke to them freely with an open heart, because it was an important way to give affection (2 Corinthians 6:11-13). He also spoke of longing for them with the affection of Jesus Christ (Philippians 1:8); an affection that needs to be mutual (1 Peter 1:7). This means that affection is given by someone, possibly a leader, and is expected to be received by a follower. How is the Leadership's affection an outward leadership attribute? The qualities of leadership affection attribute are relevant in servant leadership in the sense that they reflect the other-centered external action of a leader-servant for the benefit of others. This chapter explores these and other questions to discover the characteristics of affection attributes and to formulate a functional principle based on the expected outcome of the effective use of these attributes in leadership.

CHARACTERISTICS OF AFFECTION ATTRIBUTE

Some of the characteristics of affection can be summarized as:[12]:

- Something a person can *provide for* and *receive from* another person.
- Something a person experiences without input from any other person.
- Something that *flows and moves from* one person to another, producing some emotion;
- Something that requires *some effort* to provide such as taking care, helping, or understanding another, trying to please others, respecting their freedom, to make them happy;
- Something that *flows among people*,
- Something that one gives and *one receives*.

The functionality of this affection is that it is an outwardly directed attitude. For example, Jesus' love became affectionate when He *gave* his life on the cross for many. However, when He *wept* at the death of Lazarus, He was showing love. His love became affection when He raised Lazarus from the dead (John 11:35). In this respect, affection is more than just love for someone; it is extending a loving action, not feeling, to someone.

PRINCIPLE OF AFFECTION ATTRIBUTE

In summary, the affection attribute of a leader-servant can be characterized by the following distinguishing love-based outward qualities:

1. Affection by work done toward others' needs,
2. Affection by brotherly kindness,
3. Affection by compassion
4. Affection by practical love.

CHAPTER 2
AFFECTION LEADERSHIP ATTRIBUTE

The catalyst that initiates any affective action is the love of God and obedience to His command to love, even our enemies. Based on these characteristics, I come to the following definition:

Servant leadership affection attribute is the combined love-based work toward providing the essential help or services for the spiritual growth or survival of another person.

In this regard, affection is what a person *gives* to another based on his love for that person as an expression of love of God; it is more than what one shows to another person; it is a display of practical love at a greater level to one another. The leader may feel emotions toward a person's needs. That is just love. But the primary outcome of affection attribute is the resulting love-based emotions produced on the receiver by the direct action of the giver. This leads us to the following principle:

Servant leadership affection principle: Affection flows from a person to produce positive emotions for the well-being of another person

The principle is modeled in Figure 2, showing the relationship between the four characteristics: Leader-servant's love, kindness, compassion, and work, to the central focus of showing affection toward others, and expressed as.

LOVE + KINDNESS + COMPASSION + WORK = AFFECTION

Affective love in this expression is practical love that is given not shown or expressed. Hence, all four flow independently from a leader-servant to others or followers. The more these actions are exerted and received by the follower, the greater the emotions produced.

PRACTICING AFFECTION ATTRIBUTE

In summary of this chapter and as a practical matter, affection is something that requires some effort to provide, such as providing care, helping or understanding another, trying to please and respect others to make them happy. The level of affection a leader gives can be measured by the work done in giving and helping others to obtain whatever is needed for survival or growth. The survey a survey of 132 Christian leaders showed low agreement for the affection attribute. Thirty- eight percent (38%) of the respondents agree that they *always* influence desired change in followers by their acts of kindness (Wosu, 2014).[11] This can reflect very negatively on how members feel about the love and care from the leaders. Effective use of the affection attribute can be developed by:

1. **Giving affection by brotherly kindness.** Brotherly kind- ness as affection to another person in the form of the care and help extended to each other.
2. **Be longsuffering, bearing with one another in love.** With all lowliness and gentleness, with longsuffering, bear with one another in love (Ephesians 4:2), forgiving one another (Colossians 3:13), and submitting to one another in the fear of God. Ephesians 5:21 is a measure of our affection to bear with others in taking specific actions that make the other person feel better.
3. **Be a reflection of Jesus' brotherly kindness.** Be an example of the kind of sacrifice Jesus made as a reflection of brotherly kindness. As Jesus said, "as I have loved you, that you also love one another" (John 13:34), maintain brotherly love with each other (Hebrews 13:1), and pursue the things that make for peace with one another (Romans 14:19).
4. **Keep fellowship with each other.** Keeping fellowship with each other affords us the opportunity to know each other's needs and the affective actions we need to take to meet those needs.
5. **Readily forgive and reconcile.** Lack of forgiveness creates barriers in our abilities to extend an affective helping hand to each other. (I Corinthians 8:13; Galatians 5:13).
6. **Give affection by practical love.** Practical love given to help another is a form of affection. God's affective action in John 3:16 is a good example of agape love as an exercise of affective action for the salvation (survival) of the whole world.
7. **Providing practical expression of love to others** is the key motivator that enables a leader to selflessly sacrifice to help others in any situation. Others' focused love is affective action when a

leader looks out for what will interest and make the follower happy. (Philippians 2:3–4).
8. **Give affection by compassion.** The compassion we show to others can be a measure of our affection toward that person. With compassion and love of others, we can impact others by helping them come to Christ to receive the gift of salvation (John 14:12).
9. **Give affection by authentic affective signs.** Affective signs are things such as smiling, acceptance, commitment or promise of support, greetings, positive emotional gestures that communicate support, and commitment to helping others. Be sure to follow through with these signs!

SUMMARY 2
LEADERSHIP AFFECTION ATTRIBUTE

Before starting this exercise, please read and follow the instruction in the preface of this workbook. Answers to these questions are contained in this chapter. Completion of these exercises after reading the chapter should take 60-90 minutes.

Discovering the Leadership Attributes

1. How do we define affection? How is affective-action different from love-action?
2. How did Apostle Pau demonstrate affection in (2 Corinthians 6:11-13; Philippians 1:8)?
3. How is the Affection an outward leadership attribute?
4. How are qualities of affection leadership affection attribute relevant in servant affection?
5. Summarize the characteristics of affection by filling the following blanks: Affection is::
   a) Something a person can _____ *for* and _____ *from* another person.
   b) Something a person _____ without input from any other person.
   c) Something that--------- *and* ------------ *from* one person to another, producing some emotion.

d) Something that requires *some*---------- to provide such as taking care, helping, or understanding another, trying to please others, respecting their freedom, to make them happy.
6. How do love such as Jesus' love became affectionate? (John 11:35).
8. Based on these characteristics you discovered, state the definition of *Servant leadership affection attribute*

Principle of Affection Attribute

1. What are the four love-based distinguishing outward characteristics of affection leadership
2. What is the catalyst that initiates any affective action?
3. State the principle of Servant leadership affection principle:
4. Affection _____ from a person to produce positive _____ for the well-being of another person
5. Write down the additive law of affection leadership attribute

Practicing Affection–Attribute

1. Take the leadership Affection Attribute audit in Table 2.1.
2. What are the acts of affection attribute you display most frequently?
3. **Affection-Love-** is giving practical Love to another person for that person's well-being.
   a. How did disciples demonstrate affection attributes?
   b. How should you demonstrate love and affection?
   c. What is some practical care we can give to reach others?

Chapter 2
Affection Leadership Attribute

Table 2.1. Leadership Affection Attribute Audit					
Servant leadership affection attribute is the combined love-based works toward providing the essential help or services for the spiritual growth or survival of another person. Assess the quality of your acts of affection attribute by inserting a rating 1-5 below that best describes your response to each statement.					
Item	Acts of Affection Attribute Check 1= Always; 2= Frequently; 3= Sometimes; 4= Almost Never; 5= Never	1	2	3	4	5
1	When a person feels hurt, I intentionally and willingly show that I care for them.					
2	I make sacrifice in service to others as a reflection of kindness					
3	I give gentleness to others in the form of the care to build up					
4	I bear and keep fellowship with others in love					
5	I readily forgive and reconcile with others to the open door for wholeness					
6	The affections I give to others usually result in positive emotion					
7	My acts of care-giving are motivated by love and compassion toward others					
8	I work to help others through their challenges					
9	I give affection with authentic emotions and affective signs such genuine smiles.					
10	I intentionally extend acts of practical love to uplift others.					
	Add up your rating in each column					
Total Score	Guide and Explanation of Score: understand the areas you need to further develop			Total		
10-17	Great affectionate leader; keep it up!				
18-25	Above Average affection; need to work 25% of the areas				
26-33	Average affection; need to need to work on 50% of the areas				
34-41	Below average- affection, need to work on 75% of the key areas				
42-50	Not affectionate; Seek counseling, work in all the areas				

Table 2.2 To what level (scale 1-10) does any of the characterize your *practice* of affection leadership attribute		
	Affection leadership attribute characteristics	**Scale 1-10**
1	Affection by brotherly kindness.	
2	Affection by longsuffering,	
3	Affection by bearing n love	
4	Affection by Christlikeness.	
5	Affection by fellowship with other.	
6	Affection by Forgiveness and reconciliation..	
7	Affection by practical love.	
8	Practical expression of love to others).	
9	Affection by compassion.	
10	Affection by authentic affective signs.	
	Summary	/100

CHAPTER 3
DEVELOPING THE ACTS OF AFFECTIVE-LOVE

Affective love is the act of giving practical love to another person for that person's well-being. Affection-love is more than showing love. You can show love—such as praying for someone –without any physical connection or the person feeling or even seeing the love. The act of love that is affectionate is giving a deeper level of love in measurable terms, and it requires some work and sacrifice on the part of the giver. John 3:16 is a good example of agape love as an exercise of affective action when God freely gave His only-begotten Son for mankind's salvation (survival). The disciples also demonstrated affection-love attributes through their capacity to distribute to each other as they had needs. Affection-love can as well be measured by the work of kindness given to another person in the form of caring and helping, extended to each other, and often designed to bring emotional strength to the receiver. These actions require work and measurable sacrifices, even death in the case of Jesus. Here are some examples:

EXTEND PRACTICAL CARE FOR THE FOLLOWER

Showing practical care to each other is affective action in which a leader focuses on esteeming the followers or looking out for what will interest and uplift the spirit of the follower. This includes showing actual caring for the sick and most vulnerable further than just saying, "I love you" it is about each person, leader, and follower, humbly esteeming the other more than himself and looking outward not only for his own interest but also for the interests of others (Philippians 2:3-4). Extending practical care for the follower allows the opportunity of sharing one's self in common with followers. The disciples as leaders shared what they had with each other, provided for each other's survival, and made measurable efforts to share their possessions to render needed help. The effect of such action is that it creates a community of collegiality and a shared vision for good works. It also eliminates the possibility of negative competition or conflict as followers care for each other's growth.

BEAR WITH THE FOLLOWER IN LOVE (LONGSUFFERING)

It is usually a challenge to deal with slow starters in any organizational culture while pursuing excellence. Nevertheless, the leader-servant that looks after the most vulnerable under his or her care must, with all lowliness, gentleness, and longsuffering, bear with that follower showing love while patiently extending a helping hand to bring that follower to the desired functional speed. Bearing with the follower in love, means, readily forgiving the follower for a mistake. This will allow it to be an opportunity to use that mistake as a teaching moment; rather than a punitive moment, as much as possible. We also must be able to submit to one another, not as a weakness but as a submission to God. In this regard, longsuffering can be a measure of our affection as we bear with another in taking specific actions that make the other person feel better. It means a leader is humble enough to submit to suggestions or ideas from the follower.

SUMMARY 3
DEVELOPING THE ACTS OF AFFECTIVE-LOVE

Before starting this exercise, please read and follow the instruction in the preface of this workbook. Answers to these questions are contained in this chapter. Completion of these exercises after reading the chapter should take 60-90 minutes.

Discovering the Acts of Affective -Love

1. What is affective love?
2. Can you show love to a person with affection?
3. How did the disciples demonstrate affection-love attributes through their capacity to distribute to each other as they had needs.
4. How can you measure Affection-love in those contexts

CHAPTER 3
DEVELOPING THE ACTS OF AFFECTIVE-LOVE

Understanding the Principle of Affective-Love

1. **Affection-Love-** is giving practical Love to another person for that person's well-being.
2. What is the difference between love and affection in our context as in (see John 3:16 ?
3. Is just saying, "I love you" enough for affection? (Philippians 2:3-4).

Practicing Affective love

1. How can a leader extend practical care for the follower as an example of affection? How did the disciples as leaders extend practical love
2. What was the effect of the disciple's action on the community and their relationship with each other in their acts of affection?
3. What is some practical care we can give to reach others?
4. How can a leader bear with the follower in love (longsuffering)
5. How is longsuffering a measure of our affection as we bear with another

CHAPTER 4
DEVELOPING LEADERSHIP AFFECTIVE-KINDNESS

Brotherly kindness is not just an inward quality but is an outward quality of affection and results in the emotional strength of another person. This is very important. Indeed, it is crucial for transcendent growth and spiritual maturity for affecting how we relate to each other. Affection through brotherly kindness is required of leader-servants because it is a direct reflection of one's love and understanding of God's love, which motivates a leader to choose to serve. Love for the brethren is a distinct Christian value. Affection through brotherly kindness in action serves as a visible demonstration of devotion and unity among Christians and can be an effective way to draw others not only to Christ but to a positive leader-follower relationship.

Being an example of the kind of sacrifice Jesus made as a reflection of brotherly kindness is an essential affection. As Jesus said, "as I have loved you, that you also love one another"(John 13:34, NKJV). Our focus should fall on developing and maintaining brotherly love for each other (Hebrews 13:1). This also means that we need to pursue things that create peace with one another (Romans 14:19). Other measures and methods of kindly affection include:

Keep fellowship with each other. Keeping fellowship with each affords us the opportunity to learn each other's needs and develop affective actions that will meet those needs. The more intentional actions you take to know your brethren personally and share experiences, the closer you are and the more you can support each other in your suffering.

Readily forgive and reconcile with one another. The lack of forgiveness creates barriers to our ability to extend an affective helping hand to each other. Readily forgiving and reconciling with each other opens doors for fellowship and comfort. It also shows us how to strengthen the frail among us and allows us liberty in Christ to benefit the spiritual well-being of a weak brother (1 Corinthians 8:13; Galatians 5:13).

SUMMARY 4
DEVELOPING LEADERSHIP AFFECTIVE-KINDNESS

Before starting this exercise, please read and follow the instruction in the preface of this workbook. Answers to these questions are contained in this chapter. Completion of these exercises after reading the chapter should take 60-90 minutes.

Discovering Affective-Kindness

1. Why is affection through brotherly kindness required of leader-servants?
2. How can affection through brotherly kindness serve as a visible demonstration of devotion and unity among Christians?
3. How did Jesus demonstrate that when He said, "as I have loved you, that you also love one another"(John 13:34, NKJV)?.

Understanding the Principle of Affection-Kindness

Affection-Kindness is affection to another person in the form of care and helps we extend to each other; acts to help somebody in need to survive suffering, and, in doing so, works to build relationships with readiness to forgive offenses.

1. What two ways have you used to bear with one another in love?
2. List ways we can keep fellowship with each other.
3. How should we readily forgive and reconcile as an act of kind affection?

Practicing of Affection - Kindness:

1. Keeping fellowship with each afford us the opportunity to learn each other's needs and develop affective actions that will meet those needs. How can such action increase the closeness with each other?
2. **Readily forgive and reconcile with one another.** The lack of forgiveness creates barriers to our ability to extend an affective helping hand to each other. What is the direct effect of readily forgiving and reconciling with each other opens doors for fellowship and comfort as in (1 Corinthians 8:13; Galatians 5.13).

CHAPTER 5
DEVELOPING THE ACTS OF AFFECTIVE COMPASSION

Affective compassion is caregiving love given through acts of kindness or benevolence. The compassion we show to others can be a measure of our affection. Through compassion and love for others, we can impact others' lives by helping them come to Christ to receive the gift of salvation (John 14:12). Here are two ways we can develop or show compassion and affection:

USE EMPATHETIC COMPASSION TO GIVE AFFECTION

The act of affective compassion is to help someone in need to survive through suffering, and, in doing so, work to build relationships with readiness to exonerate each other so that we too may be forgiven by God. Born from empathy and commitment to alleviate hurt, affection from empathetic compassion is illustrated by the Good Samaritan. He showed affection through his act of empathy; he took direct and personal steps and; "went to him and bound up his wounds, pouring on oil and wine" (Luke 10:34, KJV). He provided the needed help—beyond just sympathy—for the other person to survive. This is a pure articulation of affective action in servant leadership. His emotive actions resulted in the ultimate survival of the suffering man.

GIVE AFFECTION WITH AUTHENTIC EMOTIONS

The emotions we give or receive from kindness can be referred to as affection signs. These are things such as a genuine smile, acceptance, commitment, a promise of support, greetings, positive emotional gestures, and so on, or any action we take to communicate support and commitment to help others. However, I must caution here that it is better not to communicate a commitment to help a person in a state of survival than to communicate, but not follow through. It is also better not to smile at someone in a state of suffering than give a smile that is not genuine and authentic. An affective sign has the power to help activate a positive emotional response. For example, a follower in a condition of suffering or survival mode hears a statement such as, "How can I be of help?" It recognizes this statement as the beginning of the help and healing process. In such cases, though, we must not promise what we are not able to deliver.

SUMMARY 5
DEVELOPING THE ACTS OF AFFECTIVE COMPASSION

Before starting this exercise, please read and follow the instruction in the preface of this workbook. Answers to these questions are contained in this chapter. Completion of these exercises after reading the chapter should take 60-90 minutes.

Discovering Affective-Compassion

1. Affective compassion is caregiving love given through acts of kindness or benevolence. Give two ways you can develop or show compassion-affection
2. How can the compassion we show to others be a measure of our affection (see John 14:12)?

Principle of Affective-Compassion

1. **Affection-Compassion** is caregiving affection through acts of kindness or benevolence. How can the compassion we show to others be measured?
2. The principle of affective compassion is to help someone in need to survive through suffering. How is this principle demonstrated by the parable of the Good Samaritan (Luke 10:34, KJV)?.

Practicing Affective-Compassion

1. How can you use Empathetic Compassion to give affection?
2. In the example of the good Samaritan, what was the result of emotive actions? .

CHAPTER 5
DEVELOPING THE ACTS OF AFFECTIVE-COMPASSION

3. With respect of giving affection with authentic emotions, how do we define "affection signs"?
4. What must we be careful about when we give affective signs such as, "How can I be of help?"

CHAPTER 6
DEVELOPING THE ACTS OF AFFECTIVE WORK

Affective work is intentional work done or an effort made to express any act of love to someone. The leader's level of affection is measured by that work or the efforts (giving to others, helping them obtain resources, etc.) expended in helping meet needs for the other's survival. Hence, a leader-servant provides affection when a specific work or service is completed out of love that benefits the spiritual growth or survival of another person. Here are some examples:

EXTEND AND BE SPENT FOR OTHERS

Giving affection through work also means extending, and to be spent for each other. For example, the Samaritan "…went to him and bound up his wounds, pouring on oil and wine. Then he set him on his own animal and brought him to an inn and took care of him" (Luke 10:33-34, NKJV) By setting the injured man on his donkey, the Samaritan now had to walk on foot as a way of extending himself, sharing in the man's discomfort beyond just the money he paid to the innkeeper for the comfort of this stranger whom he never knew.

Throughout the scriptures, the apostles spend and extend themselves doing good deeds and healing the sick. As leaders, it is not enough to tell your followers you love them. What efforts have you made to speak about what matters most to them? Have you made sacrifices, even if it has meant giving up some of your own rights, to support them? When was the last time you defended the interests of those, you say you love? Affection is love in action.

A CASE OF AFFECTIVE WORK

I will use the testimony already related elsewhere in another context as one example of affective work to illustrate the concept of expanding and extending oneself to show affection to a person in a state of despair.

The time to deliver our first child arrived in spring 1980. I was too excited to hold my child, while my wife was in despair as to how we would hold up financially. Furthermore, my scholarship allowance had stopped coming, and I had to take a second part-time job in addition to being a full-time student. I refused to despair. I encouraged myself in the Lord and trusted God in faith that He would come through for us.

The baby's delivery was very complicated (a story for another book), but my wife safely delivered Eliada-'who God Loves'. My wife continued to worry, and I continued to pray and hope.

"Honey, we do not have anything in the house, no baby items, no money. What are we going to do?" she asked.

"Do not worry, my wife, our God will supply," I assured her.

In truth, within me was fear mingled with excitement and hope. I resolved to triumph over the fear and focused on lifting my wife to hope in God. I remember my spirit telling me, "In all things give thanks." I did just that, by letting His joy dispel my fears. I was so happy and joyful people around me said they could feel it. My joy was more than just the baby! "My heavenly Father was too rich to leave me dry," I tried to reassure myself.

I left my wife late that glorious evening to meet the greatest miracle of my Christian life. As I got home, I realized that we had left the front door open. Before my very eyes, all kinds of baby items filled the house, everything my wife had wished and wept for, plus many more were all in the room. I could not believe it, all brand new! And, on my desk was $500 cash wrapped with a white paper that read, "To Sylvanus and Enefaa," in bold letters. More than the gifts and the money, however, was the awesome presence of God that filled that room. I had never experienced His presence in this way before. I started weeping and kneeled down to worship Him. I just did not want to stop for it was too beautiful to behold!

It was late, and I could not wait to call my wife to tell her that God had more than answered our prayers. She simply could not believe it. "Who did this and why? How did they know when to come, and that the door would be opened that day?" My wife asked, how did they know all the things we needed? Especially the very specific things my wife had just asked for less than a few hours before. These and other

CHAPTER 6
DEVELOPING THE ACTS OF AFFECTIVE WORK

questions remain unanswered even today. We never discovered who brought these items and the money to our home

As if that was not enough, a few days later, when my wife was to be discharged from the hospital, I went to the business office to sign a paper related to a payment arrangement for my wife's hospital care. I was told that the bill had been settled by someone who did not want to be identified

As you are reading this story, I hope you can just imagine the miracle and the level of affection here. Think about the time and effort of going to the store to purchase all that my wife needed, plus the time to load the items in the car, and locate our address to deliver them. And this is in addition to expending $500 on top of that! Imagine this individual driving to the hospital to inquire and pay a huge medical bill that he or she did not incur. Think about the physical and emotional energy expended to plan and work through these affectionate actions. All these good things were done by a person or persons that did not want to be identified. This is a perfect example of the servant-leadership affection attribute, which lifts up another person, with the glory going only to God.

SUMMARY 6
DEVELOPING THE ACTS OF AFFECTIVE WORK

Before starting this exercise, please read and follow the instruction in the preface of this workbook. Answers to these questions are contained in this chapter. Completion of these exercises after reading the chapter should take 60-90 minutes.

Discovering Affective work

1. How do you define affective work?
2. How can the leader's level of affection be measured?
3. The Samaritan "…went to him and bound up his wounds, pouring on oil and wine. Then he set him on his own animal and brought him to an inn and took care of him" (Luke 10:33-34, NKJV). How did he demonstrate work, kindness, love and compassion?

Understanding the Principle of Affection-work

1. **Affection-Work** is the intentional work done or effort made to show affection or any act of love to someone. In what ways can a leader himself be extended and be spent for others?

Practicing Affection-Work

1. Read the Case of Affective work. Identify actions in the case example that demonstrated the four characteristics of Affection
    a. Affection by **work** done toward others' needs,
    b. Affection by brotherly **kindness,**
    c. Affection by **compassion**
    d. Affection by practical **love.**
2. In the Case, how did they know when to come, and that the door would be opened that day?"
3. How can you describe the affective work done and impact of this miracle and the level of affection?
4. Think about the physical and emotional energy expended to plan and work through these affectionate actions. Can you describe a time you have done that for someone, what was the impact on the person?
5. Describe a time when someone did that to you, how did the affective work impact you?
6. What was the ultimate result of this act of affective love in this Case example?
7. Take the affection Leadership attribute audit in Table 1
8. Based on the questions in Table 1. can you identify each of the acts of affection leadership attribute? What ones did you score 3 ("sometimes") or less than 3? Review and learn and commit to work to improve

CHAPTER 6
DEVELOPING THE ACTS OF AFFECTIVE WORK

Table 12.2. Leadership Affection Attribute Audit

Servant leadership affection attribute is the combined love-based works toward providing the essential help or services for the spiritual growth or survival of another person. Assess the quality of your acts of affection attribute by inserting an X below the number that best describes your response to each statement.

Item	Acts of Affection Attribute Check 1= Always; 2= Frequently; 3= Sometimes; 4= Almost Never; 5= Never	1	2	3	4	5
1	When other feels hurt, I intentionally and willingly show that I care for them.					
2	I make sacrifice inn service to others as a reflection of kindness					
3	I give gentleness to others in the form of the care to build up					
4	I bear and keep fellowship with others in love					
5	I readily forgive and reconcile with others to the open door for wholeness					
6	The affections I give to others usually result in positive emotion					
7	My acts of care-giving are motivated by love and compassion toward others					
8	I work to help others through their challenges					
9	I give affection with authentic emotions and affective signs such genuine smiles.					
10	I intentionally extend acts of practical love to uplift others.					
11	Add up your rating in each column					
Total Score	Guide and Explanation of Score: understand the areas you need to further develop			Total		
10-17	Great affectionate leader; keep it up!					
18-25	Above Average affection; need to work 25% of the areas					
26-33	Average affection; need to need to work on 50% of the areas					
34-41	Below average- affection, need to work on 75% of the key areas					
42-50	Not affectionate; Seek counseling, work in all the areas					

Table 12.2. Leadership Affection Attribute Audit							
Servant leadership affection attribute is the combined love-based works toward providing the essential help or services for the spiritual growth or survival of another person. Assess the quality of your acts of affection attribute by inserting an X below the number that best describes your response to each statement.							
Item	Acts of Affection Attribute Check 1= Always; 2= Frequently; 3= Sometimes; 4= Almost Never; 5= Never	1	2	3	4	5
1	When other feels hurt, I intentionally and willingly show that I care for them.					
2	I make sacrifice inn service to others as a reflection of kindness					
3	I give gentleness to others in the form of the care to build up					
4	I bear and keep fellowship with others in love					
5	I readily forgive and reconcile with others to the open door for wholeness					
6	The affections I give to others usually result in positive emotion					
7	My acts of care-giving are motivated by love and compassion toward others					
8	I work to help others through their challenges					
9	I give affection with authentic emotions and affective signs such genuine smiles.					
10	I intentionally extend acts of practical love to uplift others.					
11	Add up your rating in each column					
Total Score	Guide and Explanation of Score: understand the areas you need to further develop	Total					
10-17	Great affectionate leader; keep it up!					
18-25	Above Average affection; need to work 25% of the areas					
26-33	Average affection; need to need to work on 50% of the areas					
34-41	Below average- affection, need to work on 75% of the key areas					
42-50	Not affectionate; Seek counseling, work in all the areas					

TOPIC INDEX

About This Book, 16
Affective Compassion, 64, 65
authentic, 19, 22
authentic leadership, 34
Authentic Leadership, 42
Authenticity, 40
Comfort, 37
commitment, 13, 20
Comparisons
  with other works, 36
credibility, 45
Discipleship
  definition of, 24
distinguishes
  a leader's act of giving, 25
Functional Definitions, 31
Generosity
  definition of, 25
Generosity c, 25
inside-out, 43
Joshua, 13
Kind Affection
  Keeping fellowship, 61, 62
  Readily forgiving and reconciling, 61, 62, 63
Kind-Affection
  definition, 56, 62, 71, 72
law of, 37
Leader as Servant Leadership, 37
  definition, 20
Leader First., 18
Leader-as-Servant Leadership, 18
leader-servant's affection-attribute
  definition, 45, 51, 56, 71, 72
leadership, **20**
Leadership Attributes, 40

Leadership Inner Value system, 20
Model, 18
Moses, 13
Navigation-attribute, 45
Organizational leadership trust, 29
Personal Outward Authenticity, 44
Practical love affection
  care for each other, 58
Practicing Servant Leadership
  Affection, 55
process, 20
Readily forgiving and reconciling
  Kind Affection, 56, 71, 72
Servant, 18, 19
suffering, 56, 62, 71, 72
test
  for leader-servant authenticity, 43
  of essential elements of personal authenticity, 43, 44
The Leadership Influence-attribute, 37W
work-affection
  definition of, 56, 70, 71, 72

REFERENCES

Greenleaf, R. (1970). *The Servant as Leader*, Indianapolis: The Robert K. Greenleaf Center

Spears, L. (1996). "Reflections on Robert K. Greenleaf and servant-leadership." *Leadership & Organization Development Journal*, 17(7), 33-35

Russell, R.F. (2001). "The role of values in servant leadership." Leadership & Organization Development Journal, 22(2), 76-83

Russell, R.F., and Stone, A.G. (2002). "A review of servant leadership attributes: developing a practical model." Leadership & Organization Development Journal, 23(3), 145-15

Terry. R. W (1993). *Authentic Leadership: Courage In Action*, **San Francisco, CA**, Jossey-Bass

George, B (2003). Authentic Leadership: Rediscovering the Secrets to Creating Lasting Value. San Francisco, CA, Jossey-Bass

Shamir, B. & Eilam, G. (2005). "What's your story? Toward a life-story approach to authentic leadership." Leadership Quarterly, 16, 395–418.

Anderson, GL (2009). *Advocacy Leadership: Toward a Post-Reform Agenda in Education*, Routledge, New York, 41

Yacobi, B.G. "Elements of Human Authenticity." http://www.philosophytogo.org/wordpress/?p=1945, Retrieved, July 15, 2012

George, B (2003). *Authentic Leadership: Rediscovering the Secrets to Creating Lasting Value*, San Francisco, CA, Jossey-Bass

Wosu, SN (2014), *Leader as Servant Leadership Model*, *Xulon Press*

González, MP, Barrull, E; Ponsy, C, and Marteles, P, (1998]. " What is Affection?" http://www.biopsychology.org/biopsychology/papers/what_is_affection.html

www.ingramcontent.com/pod-product-compliance
Lightning Source LLC
LaVergne TN
LVHW050025080526
838202LV00069B/6916

9781961526594